Lerner SPORTS

SPORTS
VIPs
MEET
JUSTIN HERBERT

DAVID STABLER

Lerner Publications ◆ Minneapolis

D0851254

Free Database Trial: **lernersports.com**

Lerner Publications Company
An imprint of Lerner Publishing Group, Inc.
241 First Avenue North
Minneapolis, MN 55401 USA

For reading levels and more information, look up this title at www.lernerbooks.com.

Main body text set in Aptifer Slab LT Pro. Typeface provided by Linotype AG.

Editor: Matt Doeden

Library of Congress Cataloging-in-Publication Data

Names: Stabler, David author.
Title: Meet Justin Herbert : Los Angeles Chargers superstar / David Stabler.
Description: Minneapolis, MN : Lerner Publications, [2024] | Series: Lerner sports. Sports VIPs | Includes
    bibliographical references. | Audience: Ages 7–11 | Audience: Grades 4–6 | Summary: "At 6 feet 6, Los Angeles
    Chargers quarterback Justin Herbert is one of the tallest passers in the NFL. He used his height and strong
    arm to become the 2020 NFL Rookie of the Year"— Provided by publisher.
Identifiers: LCCN 2022054787 (print) | LCCN 2022054788 (ebook) | ISBN 9781728490960 (library binding) |
    ISBN 9798765603994 (paperback) | ISBN 9798765601396 (ebook)
Subjects: LCSH: Herbert, Justin, 1998-—Juvenile literature. | Quarterbacks (Football)—United States—
    Biography—Juvenile literature. | Football players—United States—Biography—Juvenile literature. | BISAC:
    JUVENILE NONFICTION / Biography & Autobiography / Sports & Recreation
Classification: LCC GV939.H465 S73 2024 (print) | LCC GV939.H465 (ebook) | DDC 796.33092 [B]—dc23/
    eng/20221222

LC record available at https://lccn.loc.gov/2022054787
LC ebook record available at https://lccn.loc.gov/2022054788

Manufactured in the United States of America
1-53027-51045-2/27/2023

TABLE OF CONTENTS

>>>>>>>>>>>>>>>>>>>>>

SUPERCHARGER

Los Angeles Chargers quarterback Justin Herbert was on fire in the first game of the 2022 season. The Chargers were locked in a tough battle with the Las Vegas Raiders. Herbert was at his best. He threw a 42-yard pass to wide receiver Keenan Allen over three Raider defenders. Then Herbert completed a 23-yard touchdown strike to DeAndre Carter to give the Chargers a 17–3 halftime lead

In the third quarter, Herbert helped the Chargers put the game away with his most amazing play yet. As the Raiders pass rushers chased after him, Herbert unleashed a throw down the field to tight end Gerald Everett. A Las Vegas defender was close to Everett,

FAST FACTS

DATE OF BIRTH: March 10, 1998

POSITION: quarterback

LEAGUE: National Football League (NFL)

PROFESSIONAL HIGHLIGHTS: won the NFL Offensive Rookie of the Year award in 2020; was a member of the 2020 All-Rookie Team; was a Pro Bowl player in 2021

PERSONAL HIGHLIGHTS: grew up in Oregon; grew up with two brothers; graduated from the University of Oregon in 2019

Herbert fires a pass during the Chargers' 2022 opening-day victory over the Raiders.

so the pass had to be perfect. Everett made an over-the-shoulder catch. Then he powered his way past the defender for the touchdown. The Chargers won the game, 24–19.

Herbert's third NFL season was off to a great start. Years of hard work had paid off. He was living his childhood dream of playing quarterback for his favorite team. It was time to set some new goals, such as leading his supercharged squad to the Super Bowl.

Herbert gets low fives from his teammates as he takes the field for the Chargers.

CHAPTER 1

FOOTBALL KID

Justin Herbert was born in Eugene, Oregon, on March 10, 1998. He is the middle child of three sons born to Holly and Mark Herbert. Justin and his brothers, Mitchell and Patrick, loved football. The boys were fans of the San Diego Chargers. In 2017, the Chargers moved to Los Angeles, California.

When Justin was nine years old, he wrote a letter in school sharing his goals for the future. "When I grow up, I am going to be a professional football player," the fourth grader wrote.

Herbert grew up rooting for the Chargers, which played in San Diego from 1961 until 2016.

SUPER SPORTS SCOOP

Growing up, Justin was a true two-sport star. When he was 12, his youth baseball team played in the Babe Ruth World Series. Justin hit a game-winning home run in his team's first game.

Justin started playing youth football to achieve his goal. His dad was his coach. "We lived by four rules," Justin said. "Never give up. Do your best. Always get better. And treat people the way you want to be treated."

Justin attended Sheldon High School. He played football, basketball, and baseball. He was a star pitcher for the baseball team. Some thought he had a chance for a career in baseball. But Justin's first love was football.

He stayed focused on his dream of playing quarterback in the NFL.

In the third game of his junior season, Justin broke his leg. It was a bad injury. Doctors feared he might not play again. But Justin worked hard to recover from his injury. He returned for his senior season and threw for 3,130 yards and 37 touchdowns. He also ran for 543 yards and 10 more touchdowns. At the end of the season, Justin won the conference's Offensive Player of the Year award.

Herbert attended Sheldon High School in Eugene.

Herbert joined the Oregon Ducks in 2015.

Colleges were recruiting the talented quarterback. The University of Nevada offered Justin a scholarship to play. But Justin had his sights set on one team. He wanted to play for his hometown University of Oregon Ducks.

In October 2015, Oregon offered him a scholarship. He quickly accepted. At Oregon, Justin would have a chance to compete against the best football players in the United States.

CHAPTER 2

COLLEGE STAR

In the fall of 2016, Herbert began attending classes at the University of Oregon. He majored in science. He hoped to become a doctor if he did not make it to the NFL. But playing pro football remained his top goal.

Herbert drops back to throw a pass against California in 2016.

On October 21, 2016, Herbert started his second game as quarterback for the Ducks. The game began poorly. Oregon fell behind California 21–0. But then Herbert and the Ducks got hot. Herbert threw six touchdown passes to lead a comeback and send the game into overtime. The Ducks lost, 52–49. But their future was bright with Herbert as their quarterback.

Over the next three seasons, Herbert's play continued to improve. His best season was in 2019. He threw 32 touchdowns and led the Ducks to a 12–2 record. That included a 28–27 win over Wisconsin in the Rose Bowl. Herbert won the game's Offensive Most Valuable Player award.

Herbert's college career was over. It was time to chase his dream of playing in the NFL. But a big obstacle stood in his way. The disease COVID-19 was spreading. The league shut down, and teams couldn't meet in person with new players.

SUPER SPORTS SCOOP

Herbert was an outstanding student at Oregon. In 2019, he earned his degree in general science. He became the first Oregon player to earn the Pac-12 Scholar-Athlete of the Year Award for football.

Herbert performs drills for scouts at the 2020 NFL Combine.

Herbert kept working on his own. He set up his own practice space in a garage near the Oregon campus. He lifted weights and exercised. And he stayed sharp by throwing passes to his brothers.

"Fortunately, I've got two brothers who have been able to catch passes from me," Herbert said. "There's a big field up by my house and we're able to walk up there and go throw."

All the hard work paid off. In the 2020 NFL Draft, the Los Angeles Chargers selected Herbert with the sixth pick in the first round. He had achieved his dream. And he was going to play for his favorite NFL team.

Herbert scans the field during training camp before the 2020 season.

CHAPTER 3

ROOKIE SENSATION

Herbert arrived at his first NFL training camp with big expectations. But that did not mean he would be the starting quarterback right away. Chargers veteran quarterback Tyrod Taylor was named the opening-day starter.

Herbert did not have to wait long to get his chance. In the second week of the 2020 season, Taylor suffered a chest injury during pregame warm-ups. Herbert got the surprising news. He was starting that day against the Kansas City Chiefs.

Herbert sprints for the goal line as a Kansas City tackler tries to bring him down.

SUPER SPORTS SCOOP

Herbert stays focused on staying in shape and eating healthful food. He eats meat for protein and drinks a lot of milk. During the season, he adds more bread and pasta for an energy boost.

Herbert played well. He finished the game with 311 passing yards, one passing touchdown, and one rushing touchdown. The Chargers lost in overtime, 23–20. Herbert became only the third player in NFL history to pass for at least 300 yards and rush for a touchdown in his first career game.

Over the next few weeks, Herbert continued his hot play. His best game came in Week 5 against the New Orleans Saints. He threw for 264 yards and four touchdowns in an overtime loss. He became the first rookie in NFL history to throw four touchdown passes on Monday Night Football. Herbert won the Offensive Rookie of the Month award in September and November.

Herbert prepares to throw a pass against the Saints in Week 5 of his rookie season. He threw four touchdowns in the game, which the Chargers lost in overtime.

Herbert (*left*) celebrates a touchdown with wide receiver Mike Williams.

As the season went on, Herbert got better and better. In the second-to-last game of the season, Herbert threw his 28th touchdown pass of the year. That broke the NFL record for most passing touchdowns by a rookie. Though he normally does not celebrate on the field, Herbert enjoyed a round of fist bumps with his teammates to mark the achievement.

"I am glad we have the young man," Chargers coach Anthony Lynn said after the game. "He works his tail off. I give him all the credit in the world." Herbert finished the season with 4,336 yards passing and was named Rookie of the Year by the Pro Football Writers of America.

Herbert flings the ball over the hand of a Kansas City defender in 2020.

CHAPTER 4

WHAT'S NEXT?

In 2021, Herbert had a tough act to follow. The 2020 NFL Rookie of the Year faced high expectations after his excellent first season. But he met them. If anything, he was even better in his second year as the Chargers starting quarterback.

For the 2021 season, Herbert set a Chargers team record with 38 passing touchdowns. He became the first quarterback in team history to throw for at least 5,000 yards in a single season. His outstanding play led the Chargers to a 9–8 record. They narrowly missed the playoffs, but they were on the rise.

Herbert scrambles to avoid defenders as he looks for a target down the field.

After the 2021 season, Herbert played in his first Pro Bowl. In that yearly showcase of the NFL's best players, Herbert threw for two touchdowns and led his team to victory. He won the game's Offensive Most Valuable Player award.

In his third year, Herbert continued to improve. Though he battled a rib injury for much of the season, he led the Chargers to several come-from-behind victories. In a November game against the Arizona Cardinals,

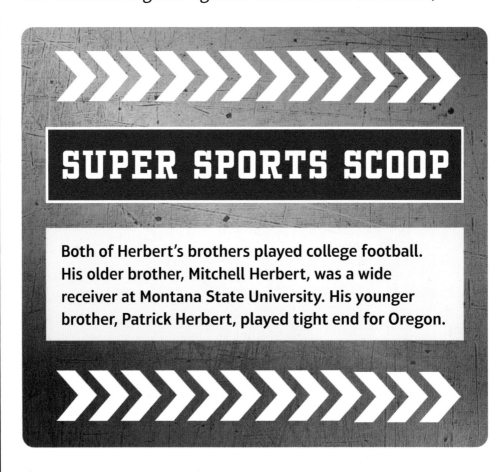

SUPER SPORTS SCOOP

Both of Herbert's brothers played college football. His older brother, Mitchell Herbert, was a wide receiver at Montana State University. His younger brother, Patrick Herbert, played tight end for Oregon.

Herbert fires a pass toward the sideline in a comeback win over the Arizona Cardinals.

Herbert threw a touchdown pass to Austin Ekeler with just 15 seconds left. Then Herbert hit Gerald Everett with a pass for a two-point conversion to give the Chargers a dramatic 25–24 win. "Big-time performance," Chargers head coach Brandon Staley said. "We couldn't have won without him." The Chargers made the playoffs. But they lost to the Jacksonville Jaguars in the first round.

Herbert keeps meeting the goals he sets for himself. Chargers fans can only wonder whether he'll one day meet his biggest goal—a Super Bowl championship.

JUSTIN HERBERT CAREER STATS

GAMES STARTED:

49

PASSES ATTEMPTED:

1,966

PASSES COMPLETED:

1,316

PASSING TOUCHDOWNS:

94

PASSING YARDS:

14,089

INTERCEPTIONS:

35

Stats are accurate through the 2022 NFL season.

GLOSSARY

draft: when teams take turns choosing new players

overtime: extra time added to a game when the score is tied at the end of the normal playing time

Pro Bowl: the NFL's all-star game

recruit: to find new players and get them to join a team or other group

rookie: a first-year player

scholarship: money given to a student to help pay for their education

training camp: a period before the start of the season when teams practice and prepare

two-point conversion: advancing the ball across the goal line by running or catching a pass after a touchdown

veteran: an experienced player

SOURCE NOTES

9   Naledi Ushe, "Justin Herbert Manifested His NFL Career on the L.A. Chargers as a 9-Year-Old," *People*, October 6, 2021, https://people.com/sports/justin-herbert-manifested-nfl-career-chargers-age-9/.

10 Jeff Greer, "Justin Herbert's Parents Write Heartfelt Sendoff Letter to Their Son," NBC Sports, June 23, 2020, https://www.nbcsports.com/northwest/oregon-ducks/justin-herberts-parents-write-heartfelt-sendoff-letter-their-son.

16 "Justin Herbert's 2 Brothers Serve as His Spotters, Receivers," *USA Today*, April 23, 2020, https://www.usatoday.com/story/sports/nfl/2020/04/23/justin-herberts-2-brothers-serve-as-his-spotters-receivers/111588046/.

23 Shelley Smith, "Los Angeles Chargers' Justin Herbert Sets Rookie Record for TD Passes," *ESPN*, December 27, 2020, https://www.espn.com/nfl/story/_/id/30607754/los-angeles-chargers-justin-herbert-sets-rookie-record-td-passes.

27 David Brandt, "Justin Herbert Rallies Chargers to 25-24 Win over Cardinals," NBC Los Angeles, November 27, 2022, https://www.nbclosangeles.com/news/sports/justin-herbert-rallies-chargers-to-25-24-win-over-cardinals/3042680/.

LEARN MORE

Coleman, Ted. *Los Angeles Chargers All-Time Greats*. Mendota Heights, MN: Press Box Books, 2022.

Kelley, K. C. *The Story of the Los Angeles Chargers*. Minneapolis: Kaleidoscope, 2020.

Los Angeles Chargers
https://www.chargers.com

Monson, James. *Behind the Scenes Football*. Minneapolis: Lerner Publications, 2020.

National Football League Facts for Kids
https://kids.kiddle.co/National_Football_League

Sports Illustrated Kids: Football
https://www.sikids.com/football

INDEX

PHOTO ACKNOWLEDGMENTS

Image credits: JP Waldron/Cal Sport Media/Alamy Stock Photo, p. 4; Keith Birmingham/MediaNews Group/Pasadena Star-News/Getty Images, pp. 6, 23; AP Photo/Ben Liebenberg, p. 7; chrispecoraro/Getty Images, p. 8; Elsa Hasch/Allsport/Getty Images, p. 9; Visitor7/Wikipedia Commons, p. 11; Brian Murphy/Icon Sportswire/Getty Images, p. 12; Brian Rothmuller/ Icon Sportswire/Getty Images, p. 13; Doug Stringer/Icon Sportswire/Getty Images, p. 14; AP Photo/Michael Conroy, p. 16; Al Seib/Getty Images, p. 17; Chris Graythen/Getty Images, pp. 18, 21, 22; Wally Skalij/Los Angeles Times/Getty Images, p. 19; Ethan Miller/Getty Images, p. 24; Tom Hauck/ Getty Images, p. 25; AP Photo/Rick Scuteri, p. 27.

Cover: Cal Sport Media/Alamy Stock Photo.